Dedicated to Marlo, Sidney, Shia, Daria and Mom.

Every night before bed, we battle each other
about who loves who more.

With this book, I'm going to prove once and for all..
that I love you more!

In fact, not only do I love you more than you love me,
I love you more than a lot of stuff!

Ok let's get started.

I love you more than...

Apples!

And you know what they say,

"An apple a day keeps the doctor away."

I also love you more than...

Baseball!

And you're good at baseball!

You can hit a home run!

I also love you more than...

Donuts!

we love donuts! we eat them all!

I also love you more than...

Skateboarding!

Skateboarding is fun! we can do tricks!

I also love you more than...

Chess!

You're good at chess!

But I'll checkmate you!

I also love you more than...

Dogs!

we love dogs!

You take good care of them!

I also love you more than...

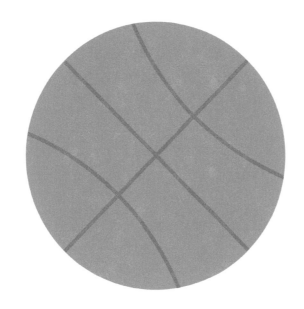

Basketball!

You're good at basketball!

But I might dunk on you!

I also love you more than..

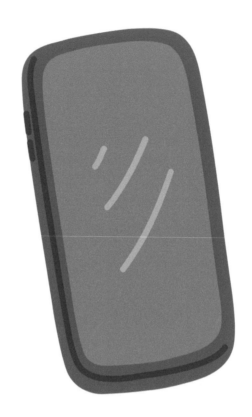

My Phone!

Not just my phone but everything on it!

I also love you more than..

video games!

And you are very good at video games like
Fortnite and Fifa!

I also love you more than..

Rabbits!

Bunnies are cute, aren't they?

I also love you more than..

Taking Pictures!

You are very good at taking pictures
with your camera!

I also love you more than..

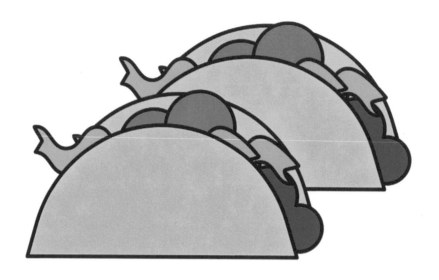

Tacos!

Every Tuesday, you eat tacos, don't you?

I also love you more than..

watching TV!

we love watching TV together, don't we?

I also love you more than..

Soccer!

You are very good at soccer!

one time, I was your coach!

I also love you more than..

work!

Sometimes, you help me with my work!

I also love you more than..

Pizza!

I don't even eat pizza any more. That's all you!

I also love you more than..

Koalas!

Koala bears are so amazingly cute!

I also love you more than..

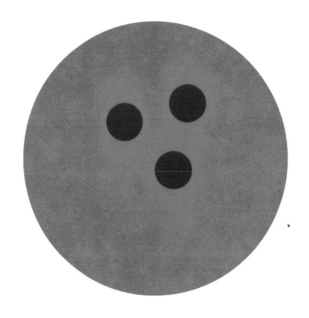

Bowling!

Let's go bowling and you can bowl a strike!

I also love you more than..

Packages!

You love picking up packages to see what's inside!

I also love you more than..

Elephants!

Elephants are such special creatures!

I also love you more than..

My Compass!

If we get lost, we can take out the compass
and find our way!

I also love you more than..

Football!

Every Sunday, you watch football with me!

I also love you more than..

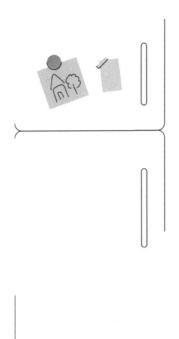

The Fridge!

You love opening the fridge to find a snack!

I also love you more than..

Giraffes!

Remember when you fed the giraffes lettuce?

I also love you more than..

candy!

Don't have too much candy! It's not good for you!

I also love you more than..

This Book!

And I love this book because you made it with me.